Gratitude journal

This Journal belongs to:

_____

_____

People i am grateful for...

Things that make me happy...

This Quote gives me strength...

"

————————————————————

————————————————————

————————————————————

————————————————————

————————————————————

"

————————————————————

because:

————————————————————

————————————————————

————————————————————

————————————————————

————————————————————

————————————————————

————————————————————

————————————————————

Today i am grateful for...

DATE / /

1

2

3

4

Today i am grateful for...

DATE / /

1

2

3

4

Today i am grateful for...

DATE / /

1

2

3

4

Today i am grateful for...

DATE / /

1

2

3

4

Today i am grateful for...

DATE   /   /

1
2
3
4

Today i am grateful for...

DATE   /   /

1
2
3
4

Today i am grateful for...

DATE   /   /

1
2
3
4

"At times, our own light goes out and is rekindled by a spark from another person. Each of us has cause to think with deep gratitude of those who have lighted the flame within us."

ALBERT SCHWEITZER

Today i am grateful for...

DATE / /

1

2

3

4

Today i am grateful for...

DATE / /

1

2

3

4

Today i am grateful for...

DATE / /

1

2

3

4

Today i am grateful for...

DATE / /

1

2

3

4

Today i am grateful for...

DATE / /

1. ~~~~~~
2. ~~~~~~
3. ~~~~~~
4. ~~~~~~

Today i am grateful for...

DATE / /

1. ~~~~~~
2. ~~~~~~
3. ~~~~~~
4. ~~~~~~

Today i am grateful for...

DATE / /

1. ~~~~~~
2. ~~~~~~
3. ~~~~~~
4. ~~~~~~

What made me smile this week?

Today i am grateful for...

1
2
3
4

Today i am grateful for...

1
2
3
4

Today i am grateful for...

1
2
3
4

Today i am grateful for...

1
2
3
4

Today i am grateful for...

1
2
3
4

Today i am grateful for...

1
2
3
4

Today i am grateful for...

1
2
3
4

"Gratitude is the fairest blossom which springs from the soul."

HENRY WARD BEECHER

Today i am grateful for...

1

2

3

4

Today i am grateful for...

1

2

3

4

Today i am grateful for...

1

2

3

4

Today i am grateful for...

1

2

3

4

Today i am grateful for...

DATE / /

1.
2.
3.
4.

Today i am grateful for...

DATE / /

1.
2.
3.
4.

Today i am grateful for...

DATE / /

1.
2.
3.
4.

What beauty did i see this week?

Today i am grateful for...

DATE   /   /

1

2

3

4

Today i am grateful for...

DATE   /   /

1

2

3

4

Today i am grateful for...

DATE   /   /

1

2

3

4

Today i am grateful for...

DATE   /   /

1

2

3

4

Today i am grateful for...

DATE   /   /

1
2
3
4

Today i am grateful for...

DATE   /   /

1
2
3
4

Today i am grateful for...

DATE   /   /

1
2
3
4

"Gratitude is a powerful catalyst for happiness. It's the spark that lights a fire of joy in your soul."

AMY COLLETTE

Today i am grateful for...

1
2
3
4

Today i am grateful for...

1
2
3
4

Today i am grateful for...

1
2
3
4

Today i am grateful for...

1
2
3
4

Today i am grateful for...

1.
2.
3.
4.

Today i am grateful for...

1.
2.
3.
4.

Today i am grateful for...

1.
2.
3.
4.

What was one small victory i had this week ?

Today i am grateful for...

1
2
3
4

Today i am grateful for...

1
2
3
4

Today i am grateful for...

1
2
3
4

Today i am grateful for...

1
2
3
4

Today i am grateful for...   DATE   /   /

1 _____

2 _____

3 _____

4 _____

Today i am grateful for...   DATE   /   /

1 _____

2 _____

3 _____

4 _____

Today i am grateful for...   DATE   /   /

1 _____

2 _____

3 _____

4 _____

"Gratitude makes sense of our past, brings peace for today,
and creates a vision for tomorrow."

MELODY BEATTIE

Today i am grateful for...

DATE / /

1

2

3

4

Today i am grateful for...

DATE / /

1

2

3

4

Today i am grateful for...

DATE / /

1

2

3

4

Today i am grateful for...

DATE / /

1

2

3

4

Today i am grateful for...

DATE / /

1.

2.

3.

4.

Today i am grateful for...

DATE / /

1.

2.

3.

4.

Today i am grateful for...

DATE / /

1.

2.

3.

4.

What simple pleasure did i enjoy this week ?

Today i am grateful for...

1
2
3
4

Today i am grateful for...

1
2
3
4

Today i am grateful for...

1
2
3
4

Today i am grateful for...

1
2
3
4

Today i am grateful for...

1.
2.
3.
4.

Today i am grateful for...

1.
2.
3.
4.

Today i am grateful for...

1.
2.
3.
4.

"Thankfulness is the beginning of gratitude. Gratitude is the completion of thankfulness. Thankfulness may consist merely of words. Gratitude is shown in acts."

HENRI FREDERIC AMIEL

Today i am grateful for...

DATE   /   /

1
2
3
4

Today i am grateful for...

DATE   /   /

1
2
3
4

Today i am grateful for...

DATE   /   /

1
2
3
4

Today i am grateful for...

DATE   /   /

1
2
3
4

Today i am grateful for...

DATE / /

1
2
3
4

Today i am grateful for...

DATE / /

1
2
3
4

Today i am grateful for...

DATE / /

1
2
3
4

Moments I appreciated this week ?

Today i am grateful for...

1
2
3
4

Today i am grateful for...

1
2
3
4

Today i am grateful for...

1
2
3
4

Today i am grateful for...

1
2
3
4

Today i am grateful for...   DATE   /   /

1 _____

2 _____

3 _____

4 _____

Today i am grateful for...   DATE   /   /

1 _____

2 _____

3 _____

4 _____

Today i am grateful for...   DATE   /   /

1 _____

2 _____

3 _____

4 _____

"Joy is the simplest form of gratitude."

KARL BARTH

Today i am grateful for...

1
2
3
4

Today i am grateful for...

1
2
3
4

Today i am grateful for...

1
2
3
4

Today i am grateful for...

1
2
3
4

Today i am grateful for...   DATE   /   /

1
2
3
4

Today i am grateful for...   DATE   /   /

1
2
3
4

Today i am grateful for...   DATE   /   /

1
2
3
4

What act of kindness did i witness this week ?

Today i am grateful for...

DATE   /   /

1. _____
2. _____
3. _____
4. _____

Today i am grateful for...

DATE   /   /

1. _____
2. _____
3. _____
4. _____

Today i am grateful for...

DATE   /   /

1. _____
2. _____
3. _____
4. _____

Today i am grateful for...

DATE   /   /

1. _____
2. _____
3. _____
4. _____

Today i am grateful for...

1

2

3

4

Today i am grateful for...

1

2

3

4

Today i am grateful for...

1

2

3

4

"In ordinary life, we hardly realize that we receive a great deal more than we give, and that it is only with gratitude that life becomes rich."

DIETRICH BONHOEFFER

Today i am grateful for...

DATE / /

1

2

3

4

Today i am grateful for...

DATE / /

1

2

3

4

Today i am grateful for...

DATE / /

1

2

3

4

Today i am grateful for...

DATE / /

1

2

3

4

Today i am grateful for...

1
2
3
4

Today i am grateful for...

1
2
3
4

Today i am grateful for...

1
2
3
4

What skills did i use this week ?

Today i am grateful for...

1
2
3
4

Today i am grateful for...

1
2
3
4

Today i am grateful for...

1
2
3
4

Today i am grateful for...

1
2
3
4

Today i am grateful for...

DATE / /

1

2

3

4

Today i am grateful for...

DATE / /

1

2

3

4

Today i am grateful for...

DATE / /

1

2

3

4

" Gratitude is when memory is stored in the heart and
not in the mind ."

LIONEL HAMPTON

Today i am grateful for...

DATE   /   /

1
2
3
4

Today i am grateful for...

DATE   /   /

1
2
3
4

Today i am grateful for...

DATE   /   /

1
2
3
4

Today i am grateful for...

DATE   /   /

1
2
3
4

Today i am grateful for...   DATE   /   /

1
2
3
4

Today i am grateful for...   DATE   /   /

1
2
3
4

Today i am grateful for...   DATE   /   /

1
2
3
4

What was the best part of the week ?

Today i am grateful for...

1
2
3
4

Today i am grateful for...

1
2
3
4

Today i am grateful for...

1
2
3
4

Today i am grateful for...

1
2
3
4

Today i am grateful for...   DATE   /   /

1

2

3

4

Today i am grateful for...   DATE   /   /

1

2

3

4

Today i am grateful for...   DATE   /   /

1

2

3

4

" Gratitude is not only the greatest of virtues but the
parent of all others ."

MARCUS TULLIUS CICERO

Today i am grateful for...

1
2
3
4

Today i am grateful for...

1
2
3
4

Today i am grateful for...

1
2
3
4

Today i am grateful for...

1
2
3
4

Today i am grateful for...   DATE   /   /

1
2
3
4

Today i am grateful for...   DATE   /   /

1
2
3
4

Today i am grateful for...   DATE   /   /

1
2
3
4

When did I feel very grateful this week ?

Today i am grateful for...

DATE   /   /

1

2

3

4

Today i am grateful for...

DATE   /   /

1

2

3

4

Today i am grateful for...

DATE   /   /

1

2

3

4

Today i am grateful for...

DATE   /   /

1

2

3

4

Today i am grateful for...   DATE   /   /

1
2
3
4

Today i am grateful for...   DATE   /   /

1
2
3
4

Today i am grateful for...   DATE   /   /

1
2
3
4

" We often take for granted the very things that most deserve
our gratitude ."

CYNTHIA OZICK

Today i am grateful for...

1

2

3

4

Today i am grateful for...

1

2

3

4

Today i am grateful for...

1

2

3

4

Today i am grateful for...

1

2

3

4

Today i am grateful for...

DATE   /   /

1.
2.
3.
4.

Today i am grateful for...

DATE   /   /

1.
2.
3.
4.

Today i am grateful for...

DATE   /   /

1.
2.
3.
4.

What made me smile this week ?

Today i am grateful for...

DATE / /

1

2

3

4

Today i am grateful for...

DATE / /

1

2

3

4

Today i am grateful for...

DATE / /

1

2

3

4

Today i am grateful for...

DATE / /

1

2

3

4

Today i am grateful for...   DATE   /   /

1 _____

2 _____

3 _____

4 _____

Today i am grateful for...   DATE   /   /

1 _____

2 _____

3 _____

4 _____

Today i am grateful for...   DATE   /   /

1 _____

2 _____

3 _____

4 _____

" You cannot do a kindness too soon because you never know how soon it will
be too late."

RALPH WALDO EMERSON

Today i am grateful for...

DATE   /   /

1

2

3

4

Today i am grateful for...

DATE   /   /

1

2

3

4

Today i am grateful for...

DATE   /   /

1

2

3

4

Today i am grateful for...

DATE   /   /

1

2

3

4

Today i am grateful for...

DATE / /

1
2
3
4

Today i am grateful for...

DATE / /

1
2
3
4

Today i am grateful for...

DATE / /

1
2
3
4

What made me laugh out loud this week ?

Today i am grateful for...

DATE   /   /

1
2
3
4

Today i am grateful for...

DATE   /   /

1
2
3
4

Today i am grateful for...

DATE   /   /

1
2
3
4

Today i am grateful for...

DATE   /   /

1
2
3
4

Today i am grateful for...   DATE   /   /

1
2
3
4

Today i am grateful for...   DATE   /   /

1
2
3
4

Today i am grateful for...   DATE   /   /

1
2
3
4

" I would maintain that thanks are the highest form of thought, and that
gratitude is happiness doubled by wonder ."

GILBERT C. CHESTERTON

Today i am grateful for...

1
2
3
4

Today i am grateful for...

1
2
3
4

Today i am grateful for...

1
2
3
4

Today i am grateful for...

1
2
3
4

Today i am grateful for...   DATE   /   /

1

2

3

4

Today i am grateful for...   DATE   /   /

1

2

3

4

Today i am grateful for...   DATE   /   /

1

2

3

4

Who helped me this week ?

Today i am grateful for...

DATE   /   /

1

2

3

4

Today i am grateful for...

DATE   /   /

1

2

3

4

Today i am grateful for...

DATE   /   /

1

2

3

4

Today i am grateful for...

DATE   /   /

1

2

3

4

Today i am grateful for...   DATE   /   /

1

2

3

4

Today i am grateful for...   DATE   /   /

1

2

3

4

Today i am grateful for...   DATE   /   /

1

2

3

4

" Gratitude will shift you to a higher frequency, and you will attract much better things ."

RHONDA BYRNE

Today i am grateful for...

DATE   /   /

1
2
3
4

Today i am grateful for...

DATE   /   /

1
2
3
4

Today i am grateful for...

DATE   /   /

1
2
3
4

Today i am grateful for...

DATE   /   /

1
2
3
4

Today i am grateful for...

DATE / /

1

2

3

4

Today i am grateful for...

DATE / /

1

2

3

4

Today i am grateful for...

DATE / /

1

2

3

4

Who was kind to me this week ?

Today i am grateful for...

1
2
3
4

Today i am grateful for...

1
2
3
4

Today i am grateful for...

1
2
3
4

Today i am grateful for...

1
2
3
4

Today i am grateful for...

DATE / /

1.
2.
3.
4.

Today i am grateful for...

DATE / /

1.
2.
3.
4.

Today i am grateful for...

DATE / /

1.
2.
3.
4.

" When I started counting my blessings, my whole life
turned around ."

WILLIE NELSON

Today i am grateful for...

DATE / /

1

2

3

4

Today i am grateful for...

DATE / /

1

2

3

4

Today i am grateful for...

DATE / /

1

2

3

4

Today i am grateful for...

DATE / /

1

2

3

4

Today i am grateful for...

DATE / /

1
2
3
4

Today i am grateful for...

DATE / /

1
2
3
4

Today i am grateful for...

DATE / /

1
2
3
4

What did I learn this week ?

Today i am grateful for...

DATE   /   /

1

2

3

4

Today i am grateful for...

DATE   /   /

1

2

3

4

Today i am grateful for...

DATE   /   /

1

2

3

4

Today i am grateful for...

DATE   /   /

1

2

3

4

Today i am grateful for...   DATE   /   /

1

2

3

4

Today i am grateful for...   DATE   /   /

1

2

3

4

Today i am grateful for...   DATE   /   /

1

2

3

4

" Gratitude helps you to grow and expand, gratitude brings joy and laughter
into your life and into the lives of all those around you ."

EILEEN CADDY

Today i am grateful for...

DATE / /

1

2

3

4

Today i am grateful for...

DATE / /

1

2

3

4

Today i am grateful for...

DATE / /

1

2

3

4

Today i am grateful for...

DATE / /

1

2

3

4

Today i am grateful for...

DATE / /

1.
2.
3.
4.

Today i am grateful for...

DATE / /

1.
2.
3.
4.

Today i am grateful for...

DATE / /

1.
2.
3.
4.

How am I better this week than I was last week ?

Today i am grateful for...

1
2
3
4

Today i am grateful for...

1
2
3
4

Today i am grateful for...

1
2
3
4

Today i am grateful for...

1
2
3
4

Today i am grateful for...   DATE   /   /

1 _____

2 _____

3 _____

4 _____

Today i am grateful for...   DATE   /   /

1 _____

2 _____

3 _____

4 _____

Today i am grateful for...   DATE   /   /

1 _____

2 _____

3 _____

4 _____

"Two kinds of gratitude. The sudden kind we feel for what we take, the larger kind we feel for what we give ."

EDWIN ARLINGTON ROBINSON

Today i am grateful for...

DATE / /

1

2

3

4

Today i am grateful for...

DATE / /

1

2

3

4

Today i am grateful for...

DATE / /

1

2

3

4

Today i am grateful for...

DATE / /

1

2

3

4

Today i am grateful for...

1
2
3
4

Today i am grateful for...

1
2
3
4

Today i am grateful for...

1
2
3
4

What activity did I most enjoy this week ?

Today i am grateful for...

1

2

3

4

Today i am grateful for...

1

2

3

4

Today i am grateful for...

1

2

3

4

Today i am grateful for...

1

2

3

4

Today i am grateful for...

1
2
3
4

Today i am grateful for...

1
2
3
4

Today i am grateful for...

1
2
3
4

" Gratitude is the sweetest thing in a seekers life, in all human life. If there is gratitude in your heart, then there will be tremendous sweetness in your eyes."

SRI CHINMOY

Today i am grateful for...

DATE / /

1
2
3
4

Today i am grateful for...

DATE / /

1
2
3
4

Today i am grateful for...

DATE / /

1
2
3
4

Today i am grateful for...

DATE / /

1
2
3
4

Today i am grateful for...   DATE   /   /

1
2
3
4

Today i am grateful for...   DATE   /   /

1
2
3
4

Today i am grateful for...   DATE   /   /

1
2
3
4

What was the most delicious thing I ate this week ?

Today i am grateful for...

DATE / /

1
2
3
4

Today i am grateful for...

DATE / /

1
2
3
4

Today i am grateful for...

DATE / /

1
2
3
4

Today i am grateful for...

DATE / /

1
2
3
4

Today i am grateful for...

1
2
3
4

Today i am grateful for...

1
2
3
4

Today i am grateful for...

1
2
3
4

" As with all commandments, gratitude is a description of a successful mode of living. The thankful heart opens our eyes to a multitude of blessings that continually surround us ."

JAMES E. FAUST

Today i am grateful for...

1
2
3
4

Today i am grateful for...

1
2
3
4

Today i am grateful for...

1
2
3
4

Today i am grateful for...

1
2
3
4

Today i am grateful for...

DATE / /

1

2

3

4

Today i am grateful for...

DATE / /

1

2

3

4

Today i am grateful for...

DATE / /

1

2

3

4

What did I enjoy listening to this week ?

Today i am grateful for...

1

2

3

4

Today i am grateful for...

1

2

3

4

Today i am grateful for...

1

2

3

4

Today i am grateful for...

1

2

3

4

Today i am grateful for...   DATE   /   /

1 _____
2 _____
3 _____
4 _____

Today i am grateful for...   DATE   /   /

1 _____
2 _____
3 _____
4 _____

Today i am grateful for...   DATE   /   /

1 _____
2 _____
3 _____
4 _____

"The more grateful I am, the more beauty I see ."

MARY DAVIS

Today i am grateful for...

1
2
3
4

Today i am grateful for...

1
2
3
4

Today i am grateful for...

1
2
3
4

Today i am grateful for...

1
2
3
4

Today i am grateful for...

DATE / /

1

2

3

4

Today i am grateful for...

DATE / /

1

2

3

4

Today i am grateful for...

DATE / /

1

2

3

4

What was one small victory I had this week ?

Today i am grateful for...

DATE   /   /

1 ~~~~~~

2 ~~~~~~

3 ~~~~~~

4 ~~~~~~

Today i am grateful for...

DATE   /   /

1 ~~~~~~

2 ~~~~~~

3 ~~~~~~

4 ~~~~~~

Today i am grateful for...

DATE   /   /

1 ~~~~~~

2 ~~~~~~

3 ~~~~~~

4 ~~~~~~

Today i am grateful for...

DATE   /   /

1 ~~~~~~

2 ~~~~~~

3 ~~~~~~

4 ~~~~~~

Today i am grateful for...

DATE   /   /

1 _____

2 _____

3 _____

4 _____

Today i am grateful for...

DATE   /   /

1 _____

2 _____

3 _____

4 _____

Today i am grateful for...

DATE   /   /

1 _____

2 _____

3 _____

4 _____

"The deepest craving of human nature is the need to be appreciated ."

WILLIAM JAMES

Today i am grateful for...

DATE / /

1.
2.
3.
4.

Today i am grateful for...

DATE / /

1.
2.
3.
4.

Today i am grateful for...

DATE / /

1.
2.
3.
4.

Today i am grateful for...

DATE / /

1.
2.
3.
4.

Today i am grateful for...

1
2
3
4

Today i am grateful for...

1
2
3
4

Today i am grateful for...

1
2
3
4

-What did I create this week?

Today i am grateful for...

1
2
3
4

Today i am grateful for...

1
2
3
4

Today i am grateful for...

1
2
3
4

Today i am grateful for...

1
2
3
4

Today i am grateful for...

1
2
3
4

Today i am grateful for...

1
2
3
4

Today i am grateful for...

1
2
3
4

"There is a calmness to a life lived in gratitude, a quiet joy ."

RALPH H. BLUM

Today i am grateful for...

DATE / /

1

2

3

4

Today i am grateful for...

DATE / /

1

2

3

4

Today i am grateful for...

DATE / /

1

2

3

4

Today i am grateful for...

DATE / /

1

2

3

4

Today i am grateful for...

DATE / /

1

2

3

4

Today i am grateful for...

DATE / /

1

2

3

4

Today i am grateful for...

DATE / /

1

2

3

4

How was I able to help others this week ?

Today i am grateful for...

DATE / /

1.

2.

3.

4.

Today i am grateful for...

DATE / /

1.

2.

3.

4.

Today i am grateful for...

DATE / /

1.

2.

3.

4.

Today i am grateful for...

DATE / /

1.

2.

3.

4.

Today i am grateful for...

DATE / /

1

2

3

4

Today i am grateful for...

DATE / /

1

2

3

4

Today i am grateful for...

DATE / /

1

2

3

4

" Gratitude is the most exquisite form of courtesy."

JACQUES MARITAIN

Today i am grateful for...

DATE / /

1
2
3
4

Today i am grateful for...

DATE / /

1
2
3
4

Today i am grateful for...

DATE / /

1
2
3
4

Today i am grateful for...

DATE / /

1
2
3
4

Today i am grateful for...

1
2
3
4

Today i am grateful for...

1
2
3
4

Today i am grateful for...

1
2
3
4

What compliment did I receive this week ?

Today i am grateful for...

DATE   /   /

1 _____

2 _____

3 _____

4 _____

Today i am grateful for...

DATE   /   /

1 _____

2 _____

3 _____

4 _____

Today i am grateful for...

DATE   /   /

1 _____

2 _____

3 _____

4 _____

Today i am grateful for...

DATE   /   /

1 _____

2 _____

3 _____

4 _____

Today i am grateful for...   DATE   /   /

1
2
3
4

Today i am grateful for...   DATE   /   /

1
2
3
4

Today i am grateful for...   DATE   /   /

1
2
3
4

"The root of joy is gratefulness."

DAVID STEINDL-RAST

Today i am grateful for...

DATE / /

1

2

3

4

Today i am grateful for...

DATE / /

1

2

3

4

Today i am grateful for...

DATE / /

1

2

3

4

Today i am grateful for...

DATE / /

1

2

3

4

Today i am grateful for...

DATE   /   /

1

2

3

4

Today i am grateful for...

DATE   /   /

1

2

3

4

Today i am grateful for...

DATE   /   /

1

2

3

4

How did I feel appreciated this week ?

Today i am grateful for...

DATE   /   /

1

2

3

4

Today i am grateful for...

DATE   /   /

1

2

3

4

Today i am grateful for...

DATE   /   /

1

2

3

4

Today i am grateful for...

DATE   /   /

1

2

3

4

Today i am grateful for...

DATE   /   /

1
2
3
4

Today i am grateful for...

DATE   /   /

1
2
3
4

Today i am grateful for...

DATE   /   /

1
2
3
4

" I've had a remarkable life. I seem to be in such good places at the right time.
You know, if you were to ask me to sum my life up in one word, gratitude ."

DIETRICH BONHOEFFER

Today i am grateful for...

DATE / /

1
2
3
4

Today i am grateful for...

DATE / /

1
2
3
4

Today i am grateful for...

DATE / /

1
2
3
4

Today i am grateful for...

DATE / /

1
2
3
4

Today i am grateful for...

1
2
3
4

Today i am grateful for...

1
2
3
4

Today i am grateful for...

1
2
3
4

Who showed me affection this week ?

Today i am grateful for...

1
2
3
4

Today i am grateful for...

1
2
3
4

Today i am grateful for...

1
2
3
4

Today i am grateful for...

1
2
3
4

Today i am grateful for...

1
2
3
4

Today i am grateful for...

1
2
3
4

Today i am grateful for...

1
2
3
4

" He is a wise man who does not grieve for the things which he has not, but rejoices for those which he has ."

EPICTETUS

Today i am grateful for...

DATE / /

1
2
3
4

Today i am grateful for...

DATE / /

1
2
3
4

Today i am grateful for...

DATE / /

1
2
3
4

Today i am grateful for...

DATE / /

1
2
3
4

Today i am grateful for...

1
2
3
4

Today i am grateful for...

1
2
3
4

Today i am grateful for...

1
2
3
4

What positive emotions did I experience this week ?

Today i am grateful for...

DATE / /

1

2

3

4

Today i am grateful for...

DATE / /

1

2

3

4

Today i am grateful for...

DATE / /

1

2

3

4

Today i am grateful for...

DATE / /

1

2

3

4

Today i am grateful for...   DATE   /   /

1 _____

2 _____

3 _____

4 _____

Today i am grateful for...   DATE   /   /

1 _____

2 _____

3 _____

4 _____

Today i am grateful for...   DATE   /   /

1 _____

2 _____

3 _____

4 _____

" Being thankful is not always experienced as a natural state of existence, we
must work at it, akin to a type of strength training for the heart ."

LARISSA GOMEZ

Today i am grateful for...

DATE   /   /

1

2

3

4

Today i am grateful for...

DATE   /   /

1

2

3

4

Today i am grateful for...

DATE   /   /

1

2

3

4

Today i am grateful for...

DATE   /   /

1

2

3

4

Today i am grateful for...

1
2
3
4

Today i am grateful for...

1
2
3
4

Today i am grateful for...

1
2
3
4

What problem was I able to resolve this week ?

Today i am grateful for...

1
2
3
4

Today i am grateful for...

1
2
3
4

Today i am grateful for...

1
2
3
4

Today i am grateful for...

1
2
3
4

Today i am grateful for...   DATE   /   /

1 _____

2 _____

3 _____

4 _____

Today i am grateful for...   DATE   /   /

1 _____

2 _____

3 _____

4 _____

Today i am grateful for...   DATE   /   /

1 _____

2 _____

3 _____

4 _____

" We can only be said to be alive in those moments when our hearts are conscious of our treasures ."

THORNTON WILDER

Today i am grateful for...   DATE   /   /

1

2

3

4

Today i am grateful for...   DATE   /   /

1

2

3

4

Today i am grateful for...   DATE   /   /

1

2

3

4

Today i am grateful for...   DATE   /   /

1

2

3

4

Today i am grateful for...

1
2
3
4

Today i am grateful for...

1
2
3
4

Today i am grateful for...

1
2
3
4

What made me feel hopeful this week ?

Today i am grateful for...

DATE / /

1

2

3

4

Today i am grateful for...

DATE / /

1

2

3

4

Today i am grateful for...

DATE / /

1

2

3

4

Today i am grateful for...

DATE / /

1

2

3

4

Today i am grateful for...

1
2
3
4

Today i am grateful for...

1
2
3
4

Today i am grateful for...

1
2
3
4

" Be thankful for what you have, you'll end up having more.
If you concentrate on what you don't have, you will never, ever have enough."

OPRAH WINFREY

Today i am grateful for...

DATE / /

1

2

3

4

Today i am grateful for...

DATE / /

1

2

3

4

Today i am grateful for...

DATE / /

1

2

3

4

Today i am grateful for...

DATE / /

1

2

3

4

Today i am grateful for...

DATE / /

1

2

3

4

Today i am grateful for...

DATE / /

1

2

3

4

Today i am grateful for...

DATE / /

1

2

3

4

What was something playful I did this week ?

Today i am grateful for...

DATE / /

1

2

3

4

Today i am grateful for...

DATE / /

1

2

3

4

Today i am grateful for...

DATE / /

1

2

3

4

Today i am grateful for...

DATE / /

1

2

3

4

Today i am grateful for...

DATE / /

1

2

3

4

Today i am grateful for...

DATE / /

1

2

3

4

Today i am grateful for...

DATE / /

1

2

3

4

" As we express our gratitude, we must never forget that the highest appreciation is not to utter words, but to live by them ."

JOHN F. KENNEDY

Today i am grateful for...

DATE / /

1
2
3
4

Today i am grateful for...

DATE / /

1
2
3
4

Today i am grateful for...

DATE / /

1
2
3
4

Today i am grateful for...

DATE / /

1
2
3
4

Today i am grateful for...
DATE   /   /

1
2
3
4

Today i am grateful for...
DATE   /   /

1
2
3
4

Today i am grateful for...
DATE   /   /

1
2
3
4

How did I show myself compassion this week ?

Today i am grateful for...

DATE / /

1.
2.
3.
4.

Today i am grateful for...

DATE / /

1.
2.
3.
4.

Today i am grateful for...

DATE / /

1.
2.
3.
4.

Today i am grateful for...

DATE / /

1.
2.
3.
4.

Today i am grateful for...

DATE / /

1
2
3
4

Today i am grateful for...

DATE / /

1
2
3
4

Today i am grateful for...

DATE / /

1
2
3
4

" Gratitude for the present moment and the fullness of life now
is the true prosperity ."

ECKHART TOLLE

Today i am grateful for...

DATE / /

1
2
3
4

Today i am grateful for...

DATE / /

1
2
3
4

Today i am grateful for...

DATE / /

1
2
3
4

Today i am grateful for...

DATE / /

1
2
3
4

Today i am grateful for...

1
2
3
4

Today i am grateful for...

1
2
3
4

Today i am grateful for...

1
2
3
4

How did I feel connected to others this week ?

Today i am grateful for...

DATE / /

1.
2.
3.
4.

Today i am grateful for...

DATE / /

1.
2.
3.
4.

Today i am grateful for...

DATE / /

1.
2.
3.
4.

Today i am grateful for...

DATE / /

1.
2.
3.
4.

Today i am grateful for...

1
2
3
4

Today i am grateful for...

1
2
3
4

Today i am grateful for...

1
2
3
4

" Gratitude is the sign of noble souls ."

AESOP

Today i am grateful for...

DATE   /   /

1

2

3

4

Today i am grateful for...

DATE   /   /

1

2

3

4

Today i am grateful for...

DATE   /   /

1

2

3

4

Today i am grateful for...

DATE   /   /

1

2

3

4

Today i am grateful for...   DATE   /   /

1

2

3

4

Today i am grateful for...   DATE   /   /

1

2

3

4

Today i am grateful for...   DATE   /   /

1

2

3

4

What made me feel energized this week ?

Today i am grateful for...

1
2
3
4

Today i am grateful for...

1
2
3
4

Today i am grateful for...

1
2
3
4

Today i am grateful for...

1
2
3
4

Today i am grateful for...

DATE / /

1

2

3

4

Today i am grateful for...

DATE / /

1

2

3

4

Today i am grateful for...

DATE / /

1

2

3

4

" Feeling gratitude and not expressing it is like wrapping a
present and not giving it ."

WILLIAM ARTHUR WARD

Today i am grateful for...

DATE / /

1
2
3
4

Today i am grateful for...

DATE / /

1
2
3
4

Today i am grateful for...

DATE / /

1
2
3
4

Today i am grateful for...

DATE / /

1
2
3
4

Today i am grateful for...

DATE / /

1
2
3
4

Today i am grateful for...

DATE / /

1
2
3
4

Today i am grateful for...

DATE / /

1
2
3
4

What made me happy to be alive this week ?

FREE GOODIES

EMAIL US:

SUBJECT: YOUR BOOK NAME

GRATIS.GOODIE@GMAIL.COM

Feedback:

hello.tdml@gmail.com

Made in the USA
San Bernardino, CA
15 December 2019